j590
REN

Renne.

Animal trails and
tracks.

$21.27

DATE			
FEB 2 1 2003			

BAKER & TAYLOR

Animal Trails and Tracks

For a free color catalog describing Gareth Stevens' list of high-quality books and multimedia programs, call 1-800-542-2595 (USA) or 1-800-461-9120 (Canada). Gareth Stevens Publishing's Fax: (414) 332-3567.

Library of Congress Cataloging-in-Publication Data available upon request from publisher.
Fax: (414) 332-3567 for the attention of the Publishing Records Department.

ISBN 0-8368-2713-9

This North American edition first published in 2000 by
Gareth Stevens Publishing
A World Almanac Education Group Company
330 West Olive Street, Suite 100
Milwaukee, WI 53212 USA

This U.S. edition © 2000 by Gareth Stevens, Inc.
First published as *Ik Laat Sporen Achter* with an original
© 1999 by Mozaïek, an imprint of Uitgeverij Clavis, Hasselt.
Additional end matter © 2000 by Gareth Stevens, Inc.

Text and illustrations: Renne
English translation: Alison Taurel
English text: Dorothy L. Gibbs
Gareth Stevens series editor: Dorothy L. Gibbs
Editorial assistant: Diane Laska-Swanke

Printed in the United States of America

1 2 3 4 5 6 7 8 9 04 03 02 01 00

Animal Trails and Tracks

Renne

Gareth Stevens Publishing
A WORLD ALMANAC EDUCATION GROUP COMPANY

This rabbit has come out of its burrow to feed. As it moves along, chewing on plants, it is leaving behind a trail of tracks.

The trails and tracks animals leave behind are signs of their presence.

entrance to rabbit's burrow

chewed food scraps

footprints

droppings

Here are some of the most common signs animals leave behind.

.⸚	tracks or prints	⊙	eggs or shells of hatched eggs
☻	food scraps	🖎	drinking or washing places
🪹	nests, holes, or burrows	�'➤	droppings
⎀	damage to trees and other plants	⸪	scents, smells, or odors
△	piles of stored food	⫽᚛	pieces of skin, fur, or bones

Animals of all species leave behind trails and tracks of all kinds. Here are some examples.

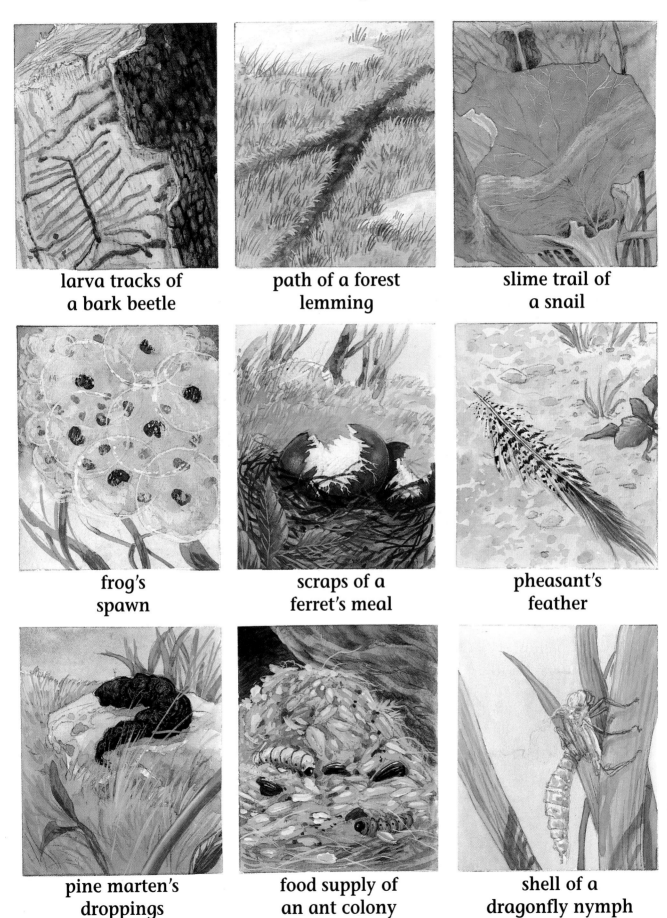

larva tracks of
a bark beetle

path of a forest
lemming

slime trail of
a snail

frog's
spawn

scraps of a
ferret's meal

pheasant's
feather

pine marten's
droppings

food supply of
an ant colony

shell of a
dragonfly nymph

Although the kinds of trails left by different species are often similar, the signs themselves can be quite unique.

scratch marks
from a tiger

prints of
a turtle

weaver bird's
nest

hatched eggs of
a shield bug

woodpecker's
holes

hatched eggs
of a rail

spider's
web

dung ball of
a heron

a wild boar's
mud hole

Trails and tracks found in the woods identify the kinds of animals that live there.

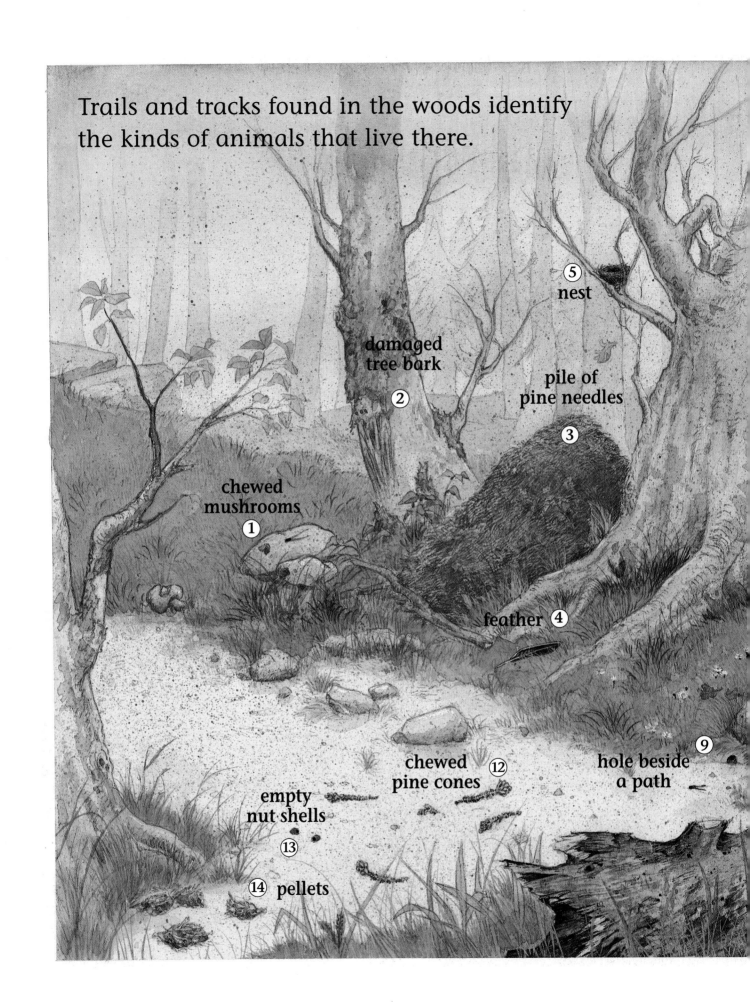

nest ⑤

damaged tree bark ②

pile of pine needles ③

chewed mushrooms ①

feather ④

hole beside a path ⑨

chewed pine cones ⑫

empty nut shells

⑬

⑭ pellets

hole in a
tree trunk ⑥

web
⑦

⑧
droppings

scratch
marks
⑪

⑩
food
trails

1.   slug

2.   red deer

3.   ant

4.   jay

5.   blackbird

6.   green woodpecker

7.   garden spider

8.   rabbit

9.   field mouse

10.   bark beetle

11.   wild cat

12.   red squirrel

13.   field vole

14.   tawny owl

Animal trails can be incidental or deliberate.

Most animals do not want to be seen by their enemies or their prey, but they cannot help leaving signs of their presence. So, they try to limit the signs as much as possible.

After carefully burying its eggs in the sand, a leatherback turtle makes its way to the sea. If the eggs are not hidden well, they could be discovered and eaten by a predator. Yet, even if the turtle hides its eggs well, it cannot hide the prints it leaves behind.

Animal prints and eggs are incidental trails.

Sometimes animals do not want to hide signs of their presence. They leave clear signs behind on purpose.

When a rhinoceros flicks its tail, it spreads its droppings over a wide area, marking its territory and letting other rhinoceroses know it lives there.

Animal scents and droppings, to mark territory, are deliberate trails.

Mammals leave trails. Their leftover food scraps and the damage they do to plants are incidental trails.

These kinds of trails usually do not put the animals that left them in danger, and the animals do not try to hide them unless they plan to return to that area for feeding.

A dormouse gnaws on nuts.

A tiger buries its leftover food.

Trails such as footprints, pieces of fur or skin, and the water or mud holes in which animals bathe are easy to recognize. Still, the animals that leave them would be in danger only if they remained in that area.

A hare leaves footprints.

A warthog wallows in a mud hole.

Because a mammal's nest or burrow shelters the animal's young and hides food supplies, it must be kept as safe as possible. The nest or burrow is almost always camouflaged so predators will have a hard time finding it.

alpine marmot's burrow

ermine's burrow

Scratch marks, droppings, and scents are deliberate trails. These signs are purposely left behind to mark the boundaries of an animal's territory and to scare off rival males, and, sometimes, females, of its own species.

A lynx deliberately leaves scratch marks to make its presence known.

To mark its territory, a musk deer leaves behind a scent called musk.

Mammals are not the only animals that leave signs of their presence. These food scraps were left behind by birds. Birds leave other signs, too.

A woodpecker
opened this nut.

A thrush got a meal
out of this snail shell.

A jay buried this
acorn for winter food.

An osprey left this
piece of fish behind.

An owl gobbled up
its prey, then coughed up
a ball of hair and bones
it could not digest.

Sparrows chewed
these stalks and
picked the grains
out of them.

Birds make holes in the ground for their dust baths. They flap around in these holes so the gritty dirt will clean their feathers.

Molting birds drop their old feathers everywhere. Birds molt at least once a year to grow new feathers.

Even with these signs, however, mammals that prey on birds have a hard time knowing where the birds are. Birds never stay in the same place very long.

Which mammals left these trails behind?

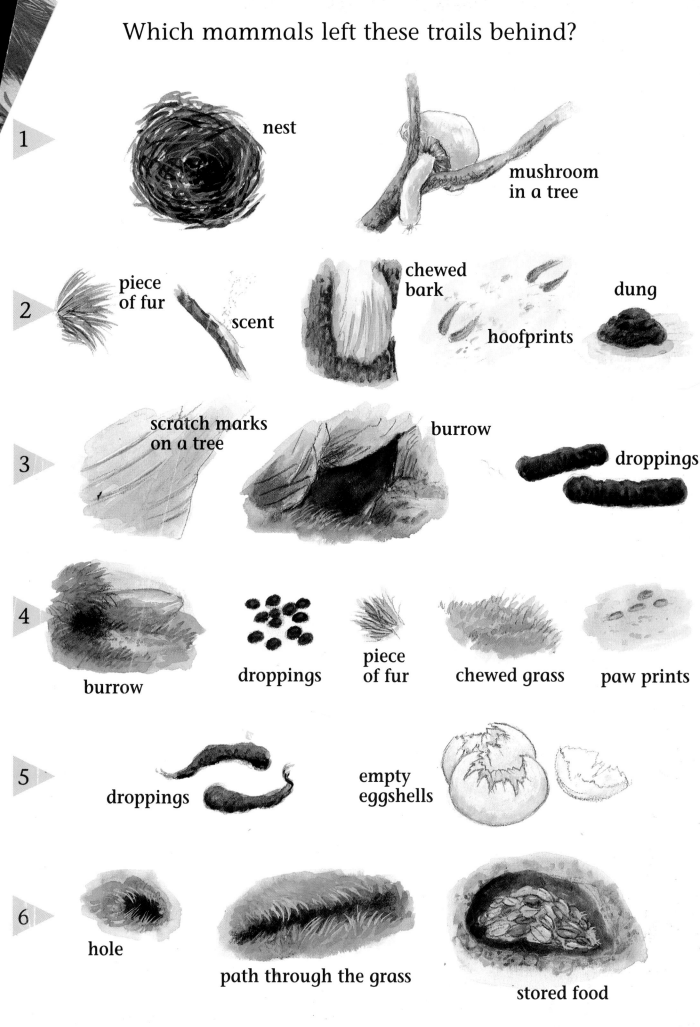

1 nest

mushroom in a tree

2 piece of fur

scent

chewed bark

hoofprints

dung

3 scratch marks on a tree

burrow

droppings

4 burrow

droppings

piece of fur

chewed grass

paw prints

5 droppings

empty eggshells

6 hole

path through the grass

stored food

① red squirrel

② moose

③ brown bear

④ rabbit

⑤ European polecat

⑥ field mouse

tracks or prints

food scraps

nests, holes, or burrows

damage to trees and other plants

piles of stored food

droppings

scents, smells, or odors

pieces of skin, fur, or bones

peregrine
falcon

great spotted
woodpecker

eagle owl

What kinds of trails have these birds left behind?

jay ⑤

song thrush ④

Legend

- .⁚⁻ tracks or prints
- ☺ food scraps
- 🌀 nests, holes, or burrows
- |ϟ damage to trees and other plants
- △ piles of stored food
- ➷ droppings
- ⫰ feathers
- ⊙ eggs or shells of hatched eggs

Male birds have their own territories, just like many male mammals. Birds, however, rarely have a body scent, so they mark their territories with their songs, instead. Their songs attract attention, too. Birds also attract attention with their colored feathers and the extraordinary ways they build their nests.

Bowerbirds build impressive arched nests called bowers. These birds leave behind many signs of their presence, including feathers, shells, and a variety of colored objects. Sometimes, they even paint their nests with the sap of chewed-up berries.

These signs help fool the bird's enemies, but, more importantly, they help attract a female bird for mating.

The way birds care for their young is quite impressive. Most young birds are frail, so their parents keep the nest well hidden and well tended. They even remove the broken eggshells and droppings of their chicks.

Birds of prey and birds that live in colonies do not have to hide their nests.

With large numbers of adult birds around, the chicks in a colony have less risk of danger. Also, the adult birds keep a close watch over the nests until the young are big enough and strong enough to leave.

The young of some bird species leave their nests right after they are born. These chicks are well developed at birth so they can move around and escape from predators.

red-legged partridge

chicken

mallard duck

greylag goose

mute swan

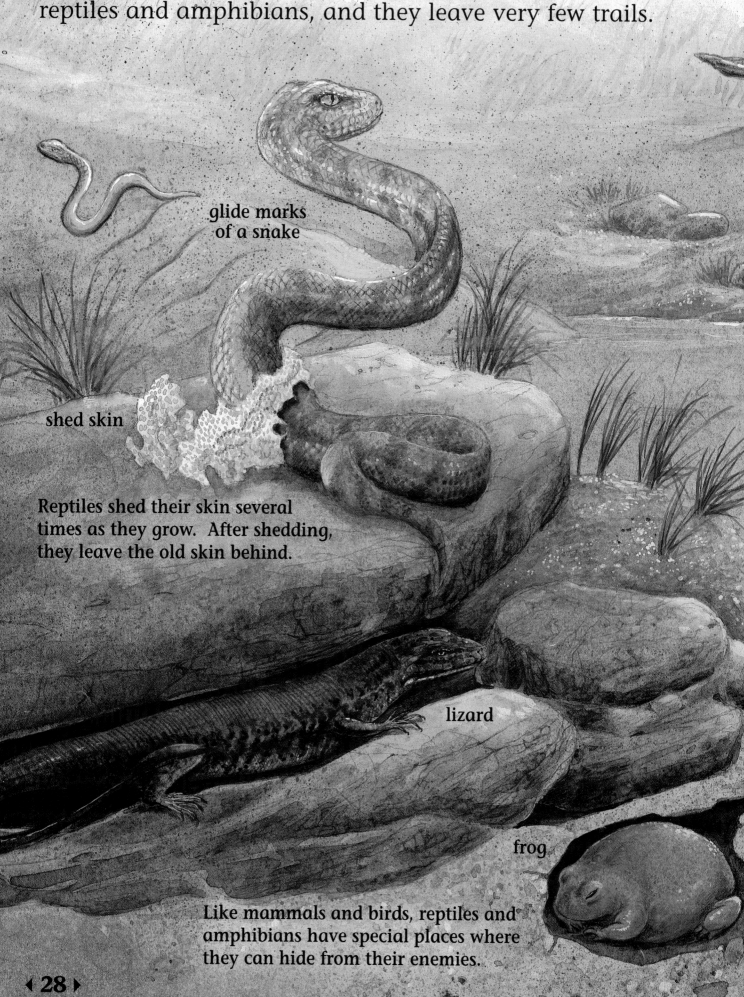

These animals are neither mammals nor birds. They are reptiles and amphibians, and they leave very few trails.

glide marks
of a snake

shed skin

Reptiles shed their skin several
times as they grow. After shedding,
they leave the old skin behind.

lizard

frog

Like mammals and birds, reptiles and
amphibians have special places where
they can hide from their enemies.

Tracks and remnants of skin, nests, and eggs are the most common signs of their presence.

crocodile's
nest and eggs

monitor's
nest and eggs

newt's eggs
and spawn

toad's eggs

Reptiles hide their nests and eggs very carefully.
Amphibians, however, often leave their eggs unprotected
in the water. Amphibians, therefore, lay eggs in large
quantities so enough young will hatch.

Insects leave many different trails and tracks, perhaps because they have such extraordinary life cycles.

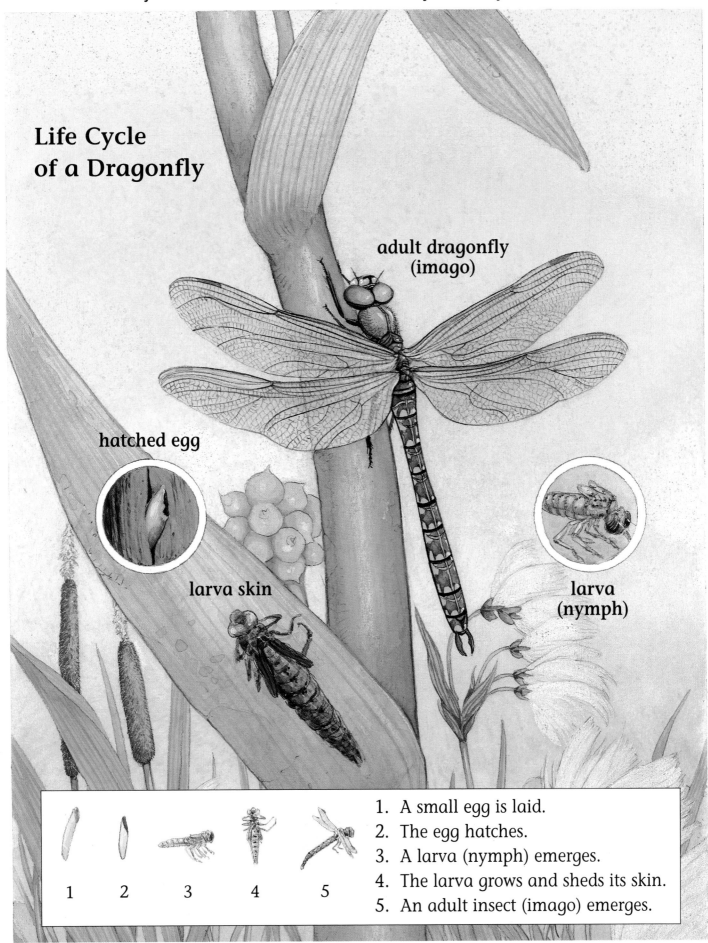

Life Cycle of a Dragonfly

adult dragonfly (imago)

hatched egg

larva skin

larva (nymph)

1. A small egg is laid.
2. The egg hatches.
3. A larva (nymph) emerges.
4. The larva grows and sheds its skin.
5. An adult insect (imago) emerges.

1   2   3   4   5

The most obvious signs of the presence of insects are the nests of social insects such as termites, ants, bees, and wasps. These insects store their food and raise large numbers of young in their nests. Some of the nests are banks or hills made of earth. Although very easy to spot, they are strong and well defended.

termite hill

aardvark

Unusual-looking mammals called aardvarks eat ants and termites. With their tubelike snouts and strong claws for digging, aardvarks threaten even the strongest and best-defended nests.

Both above and below the ground, many kinds of
small creatures, including insects, spiders, snails,
millipedes, and worms, leave many kinds of
trails and tracks. But you might need a
magnifying glass to see some of them!

1. Glowworms light up in the dark.

2. Earthworms make holes in the ground.

3. Grasshoppers hide their eggs in the ground.

4. Natural hollows hide insects and other small animals.

5. Snails and slugs leave trails of slime.

6. Glowworm larvae eat snails, then leave the shells behind.

7. Ants leave a scent behind as they follow invisible trails to find food.

8. Herbivores, or plant eaters, chew holes in plants.

9. The droppings of herbivores fall from plants onto the ground below.

10. Insects leave tracks on soft ground.

11. Dung balls are food stores for the larvae of dung beetles.

12. Spiders catch prey in the webs they make.

red squirrel

raven

coal tit

goshawk

golden eagle

red deer

three-toed woodpecker

pine grosbeak

red fox

snipe

ants

chipmunk

earthworms

centipede

◄ 36 ►

Everywhere on Earth, animals leave behind trails and tracks. Whether incidental or deliberate, each trail and track plays an important role in the survival of the animal that left it behind and in learning about the habits and habitats of that animal's species.

nutcracker

brown bear

reindeer

whinchat

wolverine

ermine

lizard

frog

Glossary

amphibians: animals that are able to live either on land or in the water. A frog is an amphibian. Adult amphibians normally breathe air with lungs, but young amphibians, or larvae, usually have gills and can breathe only in water.

camouflaged: hidden or disguised, with color, shape, or some other feature of appearance, to blend in with the natural surroundings.

deliberate: done on purpose; carefully planned or thought out.

dung: waste that comes out of an animal's body; droppings.

frail: having a weak or fragile body that might be small, delicate, sickly, or easily injured.

imago: the mature, or adult, form of an insect, especially a winged, or flying, insect; the final form in the life cycle of an insect.

incidental: happening by chance or accident and without much notice or importance, often as a result of something else happening.

larva: the usually wormlike form of a young insect, or some other animal without a backbone, at the time it hatches. A caterpillar is the larva of a butterfly or a moth. A tadpole is the larva of a frog.

mammals: animals with backbones and hair or fur on their bodies. Female mammals usually give birth to live young and feed them with milk from their bodies.

mating: a male and female of an animal species joining together for the purpose of producing young, or offspring.

molting: shedding or dropping skin, feathers, fur, or some other covering on the outside of the body in order to grow a new covering. Birds drop their feathers once or twice every year. Snakes shed their skin so their bodies can keep growing.

nymph: an insect larva that looks almost like its adult form except it is smaller and its wings are not developed. Grasshopper larvae, or nymphs, are not wormlike; they look like small grasshoppers without wings.

pellets: balls of undigested food that are coughed up by owls several hours after eating. Pellets usually contain small bones and pieces of skin and fur from an owl's prey.

presence: the fact of being at a certain place or in a certain area.

remnants: the last remaining parts or pieces of something, such as food scraps or leftovers and small pieces of objects or materials.

reptiles: air-breathing animals that have backbones and, usually, slimy or scaly skin. Reptiles move around by sliding on their bellies, like snakes, or crawling on very short legs, like lizards.

spawn: the eggs or hatched larvae of fish, shellfish, frogs, and some other animals that live in water.

More Books to Read

Animal Trackers (series). *Animal Trackers around the World* (series). Tessa Paul (Crabtree)

Big Tracks, Little Tracks: Following Animal Prints. Let's-Read-and-Find-Out Science (series). Millicent E. Selsam (HarperCollins)

The Complete Tracker: Tracks, Signs, and Habits of North American Wildlife. Len McDougall (The Lyons Press)

Everyday Life of Animals (series). Fulvio Cerfolli and Marco Ferrari (Raintree/Steck-Vaughn)

Tracking and the Art of Seeing: How to Read Animal Tracks and Sign. Paul Rezendes (Harper Resource)

Tracks in the Wild. Betsy Bowen (Econo-Clad Books)

Tracks, Scats, and Signs. Young Naturalist Field Guides (series). Leslie Dendy (Gareth Stevens)

Whose Tracks Are These? A Clue Book of Familiar Forest Animals. Jim Nail (Roberts Rinehart)

Videos

Animal Behavior and Communication. (Schlessinger Science Library)

My First Nature Video. (Sony Music Distribution)

Poop, Paw & Hoof Prints. (Silver Mine Video)

Really Wild Animals: Awesome Animal Builders. (Columbia TriStar Home Video)

Revealing Their Presence: A Video Guide to Animal Tracks and Sign. (Acorn Naturalists)

Web Sites

Appalachiantales: Animal Tracks. *www.appalachiantales.com/ animal_tracks.htm*

Nature Eye: General wildlife watching tips. *www.lindsays backyard.com/animal_tracks.htm*

Animal Tracks of Humboldt County. *www.humboldt.net/~tracker/index.htm*

Santa Clara County Parks Kids' Stuff: Whose Tracks? — The Animal Tracks Quiz. *parkhere.org/kidstrk3.htm*

To find additional Web sites, use a reliable search engine with one or more of the following keywords: *burrows, droppings, insects, molting, nests, paw prints, pellets, scats, snails, snakes, tracks,* and *trails.*

Index